Count Down To Devastation

Count Down To Devastation

Iris Charette

iUniverse, Inc.
New York   Bloomington

Count Down To Devastation

iUniverse books may be ordered through booksellers or by contacting:

iUniverse
1663 Liberty Drive
Bloomington, IN 47403
www.iuniverse.com
1-800-Authors (1-800-288-4677)

ISBN: 978-1-4401-0321-6 (pbk)
ISBN: 978-1-4401-0322-3 (ebk)

Printed in the United States of America

iUniverse rev. date: 12/08/2008

About the Author

Iris Charette is one of 8 kids her parents have.She was born with heart Disease and had open heart surgery at 13 months old.Growning up in a large family she has had her fair share of up's and down's.Poetry IS and was an outlet for Iris from the age of 13 on.Many teachers along the way have encouraged Iris to write.Some teachers played a large role in keeping her writting.She has a daughter age 9 and lives with her duaghter's father,who is a tattoo artist and artist.Iris has 9 tattoos and keeping her word to her 79 year old father has none on her arms or legs.She is one of a few inspiring writers in her family. Iris is currantly living in Lynn Ma,Usa.

Your warmth

I stare down at you
Your eyes are closed
Lips reaching for mine
Breathe hot on cold air
I feel you closing in

Your eyes open to peek a little at me
Checking to see if I still stare at you
A little smile reaches my face
I can't help but laugh
You look so sweet
So intense

Moving towards me
With a slow but steady pace
Your arms wrap me in your warmth
I feel your energy
Passing from you to me
You are like a sweet drug
Filling me with a long forgotten passion

Deep warmth
Rich inviting bath
If I was a bird
I would fly away
Just to watch you
As I flew back
Right into your arms again
Just to let you know
That I'd always come back

I never want to close my eyes
Afraid it may all have been a dream
Your warmth
Your arms
That sweet taste of your lips on mine
A dream I never want to end

I'm done

My head hurts,
And I wonder,
Why am I even here?
You don't love me, anymore!
I wonder if you ever did.
I've asked God.
Help me know what to do.
I don't want to cry anymore.
My heart is broken.
Please give me an answer!
Tell me what to do.
Maybe I was never meant to be happy.
We are not the same.
Love has faded.
There is nothing in your eyes.
You won't give up any bad habits.
My sadness cuts deep into my soul.
I've tried to be the woman,
You want me to be.
I hate the way your eyes look when you're high.
You smell like an ash tray.
Breath comes out, fills the room with smoke.
You leave a dirty smell on me when you're near
You look stupid drunk,
With stars in your eyes,
That guilty smile on your lips.
I dream of your grave.
The hole I would love to dig.
I wonder why God hasn't taken you away.
You make me nuts.
Like I have mush for brains.
I'm so sick of the roller coaster,
You put me on.

I'm sick from the highs and lows.
If I could,
I'd bury you
Toss dirt into your grave with spit.
I hate you!
I almost wish I was done

In my dreams

Lost in thought,
 It's all about you.
Wondering why I even think about you?
I want; I need to close my eyes.
Fearing you'll be in my dreams.
Not loving you and not sure what I feel.
Can I keep this up?
Hate you some days,
Wishing for more,
Knowing it will never happen.
Why do I feel this way?
I just want to close the door,
Build up walls again.
Breathe or die trying!
Not wanting to share you with anyone.
I'd lock you up in a room.
That I only have a key,
See, feel, hearing you,
Your touch is reaching for me.
I need to listen to myself.
My heart has the answers.
Never truly having you,
It's only in my dreams.

Within me

Breaking like thin ice,
Like On a warm day.
It is like winter and the coat you put around me.
 Sunny days now need it less.
Soon I won't need that ever again.
Maybe the warmth will reach me.
I feel you.
Touching like a piece of heaven.
The cozy comfort of this warmth
It's deep in my soul.
I breathe in and out,
The smell,
It's my dislike of your cigarettes.
When it comes to me,
 It no longer stresses me out.
I feel your breath on my face.
You're Arms circling me.
The pressure I feel on my lower back.
I lay my head on your chest.
I breathe you in again.
Dream the sweet awful serenity.
Your heavenly being is, within me.

Your Dreams

I hope you find yourself out there.
Lost and your trying to fit in.
Reaching your dreams
Lost along the way,
Doing what is right,
So hard
But loving you more inside
I know how to show you.
I hope you find yourself now.
Needing it more then I do,
I wish you find what you're looking for.
Just know I love you.
I love the way you stare while you're working,
The way you hold that paint brush in your hand
You see what others only dream,
The way you tattoo my back
Leaning in
Breath on my skin
Sending chills up my spine,
I love the way you see me
The way you hug me and hold my hand,
I love the eyes you hide beside your glasses
Your love makes me feel
Like I'm never alone
How can I hold you back?
For the road
It calls your name
Like souls call mine in the dark.
You have to go
I will let you know,
When I want you back
I love you.

At Night

I miss you
Dreaming about you
In your arms
I lay
Warm in your embrace
I dream about you late at night
Your arms around me
I feel them circle me
I keep dreaming
Every night
I feel you
Wishing we could
Lie together.

I have no answers

I opened up to let you in
Realized what I have done
Trying to push

Wanting to close a door
I had left open
You walked in
Welcome at first

Confused by my sudden change
Fear out of no where
Of the what ifs

Mending my broken heart
Torn by my own hands
I have no answers
Sorry for all I have done

Finding Love

A hand brushed back my hair
Tucking it behind my ear.
Fingers run softly across my check.
Eyes locked on mine.
A slow smile teased his face.
I look deeply but shyly at him.
Eyes squint at me and with a glow in them.
Blood runs up and down me.
Warming my body in a hot,
Chill of fire and ice.
I fear the hair on my arms rising,
 Close to goose bumps.
I look away for a moment to grasp something,
Other then every thought I have of him.
I can't help looking up again.
Eyes wait for my return.
The smile that so tried to be controlled,
Gives way and floods my face.
I'm a fool in the court.
I raise my chin,
Showing how it doesn't affect me.
Eyes laugh at me,
I fail and look away again.
This time when I glance back,
Hands grab my face.
He bends towards me.
I lean more then I mean to,
Right into his arms,
All the way into meet him.
We kiss and I can't breathe.
I no longer wish to breathe ever again.
My heart races my head numb,
When released I can again,

I am filled with warmth,
  From his lips.
As soon as the kiss is over,
Shyness sets in.
I wish for it all over again
Love can come in a moment,
When you lest expect it,
It finds you.
When you weren't trying to lead it in any
direction,
Love is in your heart.
Even when it's not suppose to be that way.

My Love

With open arms,
I take you in.
Wrapping my self around you,
Your fire reaches me.
Heat becoming one,
Are breathes combined.
Souls cresting each other,
Minds locked together.
Same thoughts reach each other.
Faint heart is warned!
Love reaching untouchable understandings,
Blocking out the world,
Making one of are own.
Eyes reaching beyond the surface,
Are depths reachable only by us!
Envy, jealousy and a few more deadly sins,
 Have all been directed at us.
Closed up in are own world,
We don't feel their pain.
We brace are self against each other,
Holding, supporting and comforting,
Working together as one.
You are my love.

Unknown Secrets

I lay deep beneath my covers.
Trying to hide,
 Pretend that I am ok!
Hating the way I feel!
Lost in my own emotions
Crying inside!
Disliking what is coming out.
Rage, anger, hate
And detesting the way I feel.
 Wanting it to stop!
The pain hurting so much
Crushing my chest
One tear runs down my face
Leading to more
Unable to stop the water fall
Who is this person?
Why do I feel this way?
Just take this pain away!
I never want to love again!

The Shield

I raise my shield; pull out my sword, and Lashed
out.
My sword jabs and crosses over my enemy.
With each swift movement leaving wounds!
I hurt or be hurt, runs through my mind.
Fail and be the one that walks away wounded.
Even scarred, if my enemy is good.
The shield comes up higher,
Remembering, not to let it fall,
Hiding behind it, I feel safe.
For a moment I feel confident,
And think it's best to attack.
I strike out, lunge and jab.
My target reached,
The perfect hit.
The wounded walks away.
Licking his wounds,
I hold my sword up,
Shield still in place.
I watch the wounded.
Fearful of another attack,
Waiting for the withdrawal,
For the break down,
A hopeless failing expression.
With relief I put down my sword.
I disarm my self. And I breathe.
Then I cry.

Sleep

The intake of my breath
Slow and steady
Wind cool and sweet
Across my face
Down my throat
And into my lungs
The smell of my room
Familiar and comfortable
Warm inviting, renewing
The safety net here
Only I can see
My covers full and heavy

Each to its own comfort
Within their room
Different but all the same
Where we all sleep
Is are home
My breath released
Pillow reaches for my head
Sleep within me
I close my eyes
Dreams come forward
I breathe in and out.

A New Home

My eyes are closed
I see black
Little flashes of color
Runs across the black empty space
The outlines of windows appear
I know the change in my heart
It always comes
Each shape revealed
To a place, a time
Visions always come
Before the day
I'll know when I enter that house
When I walk into that room
This will be my new home
The place I'll live till that day
I close my eyes
I see black
Then flashes of light and color
The shapes will come.

Still bitter

Angered by your lack of love
Your fake jokes, smile that meant nothing
How you lied about caring
Makes me sick!
You never loved me!
You loved the idea of me
Looking for a woman, who you think needs you

You were never crazy about me
You are full of it
Your lies are over
It was all a mistake

 Chest feels heavy, lungs weak
Hands shaking, palms sweating, ill inside
Lost for words, close to tears
I feel my fears

Understanding who I am
Not knowing myself
I close my eyes slowly
Breathe in and out
My eyes lids feel heavy

Is this the end?
Am I happy or am I sad?
Did he love me?
Maybe the thought of me!

I pushed him away
Like I did them all
God I hate these stupid walls.
Relationship is towards, it's end
Unfixable at this point
Feeling like it was not just my undoing

What happened to are dreams?
The love I thought you had!
Where did it all go?
When did you fall out of love?

Alone in my own head
Feeling bad about everything
I thought we were meant for each other
I was wrong
The woman you dream of doesn't exist
Every woman has her moody sides
You are more in love with your dog
Then any woman you ever met

I feel empty
Not in love
Not even sad
I sit here
I wonder if you ever loved me.
Was I important at any point?

For two nights I've cried myself to sleep
I'm not sad
I hate you

Your lies will catch up with you
You are crazy about your self
Not me or love
Your games will get old
The people who love you will see you
For whom you truly are
Your patterns of lies that fakeness will be revealed
All who believed in you, will question who you
are
Your bed of lies will eat your skin raw
Be red, blistered and the rash will spread
Hopefully it will spread to your face
Where it will eat your face to the ugly face you
really are

I don't hate you
I wish you to hell
To hell with it all
I'll never marry again

The wrong man

I've been crying everyday
I question if I ever loved you
So desperate and depressed
Sense I left you

I wonder what you told
That other woman about me
I remember all the things you told me
About your ex girlfriends

I realize now
Maybe it all wasn't true
You could have made up
Half the things you said
Changed it all around
To look like
The good guy

Knowing you now
Being one of them
Another one of your ex-wives
I realize that most of it
Must have been lies!

What kind of man
Takes a woman
To all of his
Ex-girlfriend's
Favorite spots
Why eat at the same diners?
Climb all the same rocks and hills!
How can waterfall
Still be so beautiful,
After taking so many women there
With you?

When we stood there
Who were you really thinking about?
I'm guessing it wasn't me!

All your old stomping grounds
Taken with 4 wives
And countless girlfriends
You pointed out every spot
With another woman in your arms
A bridge you got married on
A river you swim
All with another woman
At every bend

This one hated the water
That one hated the walk
She never made it to the top of the hill
Never looked over the waterfall from this point
But she stares at the same place
And that one hugged you there

I never had a chance
With all that history
From your past!

I had to break away
Really see what I had done
You were the wrong man
And I have hurt the one
I really loved
You are not that man
You're not the one

The one I love
I hope he forgives
For what I have done with you
This was one of my biggest mistakes
Of my whole life!

I should never have been
Your wife!
I should have taken
Another man's name!
I only hope
This hasn't made
And unforgiveable
Strain on are relationship
My life will never be the same

I only hope
He forgives
And makes me his wife

I love him, not you!

I realized today
That it is really over
The hurt is so deep
Almost unbearable
Soul wreching thoughts
Across my mind
I keep remembering are talks
Dreams and ideas
The thoughts of
What, are old age would be like
What I thought I wanted
Was all in you

Just when I think I'll break
Never be put back together again
So much understanding enlightens me
I realized it's over
I have walked away
Understanding more about me
When you opened up
It has become clear
You have walls too
Just as I do
We both wanted love
But don't even love are self
More then understanding
You wanted that fairytale
That pixy dust
That makes everything magical
The blurry glowing light of happiness
You believed in those children stories
That the prince and the princess
Live happy ever after

A little odd for a man
To believe in such crazy girl things
How life would be, so easy!
If love was never ending
Only if love fixed everything
Voices never rose
Nothing ever came out wrong
Hurtful things never said
Because love is always there
But it's not that way
Love doesn't keep you in the clouds
It doesn't make everything right
It is the most misunderstood feeling
Of them all
Maybe the layers of love
Is what makes the happiness?
Like a mother who lets her child fall
Lets her child know right from wrong
Love has lows and highs
What I saw in you
Your walls
I have seen in me
Trying to love you
Has made me understand,
Me!
By understanding you!
Are relationship maybe be over
The marriage may have fallen apart
But I have gained more then I have lost
I found me
Through my tears
My eyes have opened up
What I see
You have not gained
I have had love all along
A friend, a love, a man

Who understands me?
I just didn't see him
Looking past him for the greener grass
On the other side
He is here
To pick up the pieces
That you made fall
Always forgiving and understanding
Pointing out what I can't see
He has helped me sort through
What I have learned
Being with you
I may not be perfect for you
We have hurt each other
In are search for love
But my love has opened to a new old love
I am perfect for one man
That one man is not you
It's a man who has seen me for years
I love him more
Then
I have ever loved you

Tell me

Don't ask me if I'm ok
Ask me if I want to talk
Don't tell me I'll be fine
Or it will get better
Tell me the truth
Tell me you have
Been here
Tell me the hate and sadness
You have felt
Tell me what has made you smile today
Why you laughed!
When all you wanted to do
Was cry
Tell me
I'm pretty
And a good person
That I have done a good job so far
Tell me you will be my friend

Don't say goodbye

My mind wonders off in a different reality
My eyes focus on something not there
I don't see what I'm staring at
Where have I gone?
Remembering it all like it is yesterday
All the old emotion coming back to me

I hate you
I hate you
I hate you

You're doing it to me again
Away on your own
Trying to make it big
Working on you
But really I love you!
What about us?

Home alone again waiting for you
Trying to decide
Where we will live
How will I make it on my own?
So scared inside
Alone
All on my own
Staying here in our apartment
It all comes back in a flood of emotions
I feel you leaving again in my mind

Don't make me regret this moment
I can't handle a big good bye
I don't want to cry
Kiss me, hug, just smile and walk away
Don't make me cry!

I don't want to regret this moment
I shouldn't have to say goodbye

Stay here
Things will get better
You don't have to work so far away
You can make money at home
Is the money so much better so far away?

A tear rolls down my face
Waking me from my daydream
You have already gone
Been gone for days
Maybe it's already been a week
Time slipping away
As I wait
For you to come back

To my friend

When you hate me
I hate me too
When you smile
I smile too
If you cry
I've been crying too
When you whisper to your self
I hear your words
Like they have been spoken in my ears
When you dream
I've been dreaming too
When you need a hug
I will give you one

Love me

I've wrote you letters that I never sent.
I dream at night, of you there
I hug, a man that I love
In my dreams
You kiss me, we make love!
I smell your hair
Lay my head on your chest
You rub my back
I feel blessed

Love me like the sky loves the moon
Like the stars do the night
Light up my life
Whisper sweet words in my ears
Not the nothing that makes me fear

Wash away my worries
With dreams and hopes
Don't make me feel
Like
I am a joke
Take my hand and mean it
Warm my soul with hugs and kisses

Don't make me hate you
Don't tell me to do dishes
Tell me, you love me
I'll know it's true

Confused

You make me angry
I want to take my frustrations out on you
Why do you say the right things
To set me off
You know the right words
It's like you want
To push my buttons
The joke is on me
It never was real
I must have been fun
To toy with
I wish I knew what you had said
The phone kept breaking up
I didn't catch every word you said
Now our relationship is over
I'm left to wonder why

A poem for you

This poem is for you
You know who you are
You hurt me
And left a scar

I opened my heart to you
Let you in
You took from me
Part of my passion
That I held deep inside

This poem is for you
Hope you know
What I felt was real
And true

Break a woman's heart
Feel her pain
You'd never be the same

I'm glad you could just walk away!
My pain is here to stay
I'll get over you
You're just like the rest

A cold hearted snake
With no shame
They make break up songs
About men like you
So women like me
See their mistakes

If you are unclear
That this poem is for you
Let me enlighten you

I wish you lots of bad luck
Someday you'll see this poem
Know I was falling in love with you
All you'll have now
Is this poem
Not a shred of my love

For your head

I'm listening
You're talking
My ears burn
At your words
Controlling my emotions
I shake my head in agreement
Not able to tell you
How I really feel
It would upset you
If you only knew
Not agreeing to everything
My head hurts
So yours won't
More giving
Then I ever have been
Understanding more
Then you think
How I wish
I could
Communicate
How I truly feel
One day when you heal
I'll say it all
These unsaid words
You will be shocked
Why do we play
These games in life
Play along it's all a game
How I never understood
These words
Till now

Love and friends

Are love has become
What I never thought it could
Beyond loving
More of loving friends
Best friends with more to share
Our daughter an unbreakable bond
Both reaching for unseen dreams
An invisible line connecting us
To each other
Hidden from most eyes
Shared past and paths
Taking each other for the ride
Hoping to reach an unseen goal
Encouraging each other
To succeed
Never wishing the other to fail
Hope
That when we reach for
All we have dreamed of
Is still in each others arms
May the road take us both there
If not with love
Then a friend instead

Always wanting you in my life
Never without doubt
That we won't get everything
As long as we have each other
Please take my hand
Say you love me
Not wishing me unwell
If you should

Never get all you want
I hope you will still care
About our friendship
If unable to love again
Don't lock me out
For all I have said and done

I don't know

I'm afraid of it all
Of being in love
Marrying again
Opening up
Not shutting people out
Letting anyone love me
Believing I'm worth it
Knowing I want it
Wondering if I'll hurt you
Knowing I could
Confusing myself
Questioning what I'm doing
Thinking you could be right
Maybe wrong
Where is any of this going?
Lost in my mind
None of the question ever being answered
Already I am breaking
As you plan to walk away
Sorry for everything
Regretting it all
Wanting it more
Justifying your better off
Without me
You deserve more

You are what you should be

In my eyes
You are
What
You should be
I regret everything
That smile
Your jokes
Our walk on the beach

More

My breath comes in slowly
I feel it heavy on my chest
I find myself sighing
A little numb from thoughts
I'm opening up to you

I sit here
Wondering if that's a good idea
Why do I want to know,
How it will end?
Not thinking about
Maybe there is no end
Just a beginning
A life time of happiness
Waiting for the taking
Opening new doors
Dear I dream
Hope for more
Not any of this
Sad existing
Day in, day out
Same thing
Nothing more or less
Why can't I be happy?
Am I capable of it?
More then this
Happy but worried

I stare at the floor
Like some kind of answer
Will pop up from the wooden floor boards
Staring at the cracks
Like they have undying wisdom hidden beneath

I don't think you have the answers
I know, I don't
There is a fan going in the kitchen
But it's not very hot
To lazy to get up
And turn off a ceiling fan
More in a mood to fall asleep
Finding answers in my dreams

Such a small apartment
So boxed in
"I need higher ceilings"
Like that crazy movie said
That I watched last night

I really should clean
But it's so boring
I'd rather sleep

Day dreaming
Like I have a right
Because there is nothing for me to do

What a joke I am
A lonely mother
Who is taken care of?
I just should do my part
Clean the house
Make the dinner
Save the money
This is a life you would have to want
To be happy
With what I have
I dream of being a mother, wife and more

My heart still beats for yours

You think your friend is gone
Are love has faded in your head
My heart still beats for yours
It will till the end
You get disappointed in me
What you think you see
I love the little things you do
The person who you really are
I understand your thoughts
Better then my own
I think you need to give us time
It will work out in the end
If you believe everything happens for a reason
We will be fine
I may be harsh with words
Unkind at times
But I love you with all my heart
Even when we are apart
Others may not understand you
Wonder what I see
Some of your best qualities
Makes you a perfect fit to me
You're a dreamer just like I am
You make decisions with your heart
You go where you think you fit in

Your eyes always scan a room
As you enter it
Your love for art
And the way you think
Makes me fall deeper in love with you
But one of the best things
I love about you
You're bored with an ordinary day

Writers block

My mind blocked
Writing unbearable
Thoughts overwhelming
Where do I begin?
At what point do I give up
A novel, a dream
Which story do I start?
Titles flow out of my mind
Chapters unwritten
Time not on my side
Deadlines I never could make
The untold story
I've yet to write

My emotions on edge
Feeling ready to erupt
Yet I must not give up
The stories are inside me eating away
Like a parasite
I'm the host and it's living off me
I can feel it inside
Wanting to come out
It has been in there long enough
It's ready to find
Its way out
Will it kill me?
 In the end
Or
Will I
 Finally write

Reality

My mind wonders
Off in a different reality
My eyes focus on something not there
I don't see what I'm staring at
Where have I gone?
Shadows in every corner closing in
I try not to see them
With unopened eyes
I know their watching me
Trying to drive me crazy
Maybe they envy me
I don't understand
What it is they want
Trying to haunt me in the dark
I sleep less then I should
I try to understand
What I know I can see
My arms are full of my own load
I can't take these silly shadows
Their eyes are on me
Just when I think I will scream
I hear a dog bark
An ambulance drives by
I'm woken from my Trances
I see nothing wrong with the room
I'm back to a normal reality

Sister

I wasn't one to stand out in a crowd
Never the center of attention
I wasn't one with all the good looks
God gave that to my sister
But I loved her anyways

We were singing with the radio
Taping our favorite songs
But she was the star

She danced around her room
Holding her brush like a Microphone
Watching herself in the mirror
Singing, smiling, dancing,
 Like no one was looking

We are like best friends
More then just sisters
Not a care in the world
Loving being young

How things have changed
Now grown up and mother's
Stressing over normal days
Working off and on when needed
Miles between us
Not in the same state
Just an email or phone call away
Still close sisters

We may not see each other everyday
We sometimes have no time for the phone
But nothing will come between us
Best friends
Sisters

A poem for Joe

I sit alone again
Wondering why you have left
Always looking for what is right here
My love means more
I wish you could understand
I wait again for you to miss me
And wanting to come back
Using me as an excuse
For things not working out
Really it's just you
Wishing you could have, what you don't
It may make sense if you listen to your heart
Knowing what I do and you don't
Wishing I could give you the answers

I would build you a million tattoo shops
If you would stay home with me
But your heart doesn't tell your brain
It's me you really need
Not the miles money or fame
It's all the same
Without love it means nothing
Who inspires you to do your best?
Never letting you give up
Why can't you be happy here?
With just my love

Broken

Why these holes
Missing pieces
Puzzles never complete
Always looking
No answer
To my questions
Void in my heart
Voice without a face
Knowing something is wrong
Why do I pray for a miracle?
But don't know what I'm asking for
People hurt
Faces sad
 To a wrong path again
God give me a sign
Let me know where
I should go
Answers the questions
I don't even know
I'm asking
Heart broken
Before anyone has tried

Broken, Crack, shattered

Hurt to many time
Afraid to let anyone in
Lost in my own mind
Scarred deep within
Broken
Heart never truly mended
Cracks
Like a shattered window
To many pieces
Like a vase that a child breaks
Trying to fix before mom gets home
The glue too visible
Just doesn't make a perfect fix
A door used on the wrong doorway
That will always not close right
A car with a bad body job
With the used car sales man
Lying to get it sold

Never will I be the same
I'll always feel the pain
My eyes will give me away
Show my soul

Sorrow they will see
Hurt feelings, unloved
Trash me, call me names
I'm stronger then most have to be
Judge me
I'll make the finial judgment

I know who I want to be
You can close the door on me
Even lock it
I won't let you through out the key
My dreams of being, doing and seeing
Are up to me
They say when one door closes
Another will open
I don't care if your not there in the end
Maybe you were not a true friend
I love myself as much as I hate you
That's what holds the balance of me being me
Understand or don't!
That's up to you!
Cracked
Shattered
My soul is mine to break

Questions

When will we talk again?
How will I fix it?
I opened my heart
Let people in and hurt
The crash of emotions
Falling from high heights
Why do I feel alone?
How can I open up again?
Who wants a broken soul?
Lost and confused
In need of repair

Fighting

I can't deal
This is too hard
I don't feel worth this
To many questions
A mind filled with doubt
My heart to weak
Soul full of sorrow
Ears that don't listen
I walk away when I have to
I can't fight every battle
Winning was not my plan
You can't understand
I don't understand my self
Your heart isn't big enough
To fit all of me in
My dreams are
Beyond common wanting
I need too much
If you think you're ready
Then let us begin

Autumn

My love for you is like
The season I love
Colorful like the leaves
On the trees
Warm days start out
With a light wind
But like are love
An autumn day
You never know
How it will stay
Warm days turn into cooler ones
The leaves so beautiful
With red, orange, yellow and green
Turn brown
They fall to the ground
The coldness makes you
Want to put on a sweater
Like are relationship
 I put walls back up
Needing protection from the coldness
I can feel coming
The cold reaching
Deep in me
Like the cold air
Breathing taking a different turn
Like the wind steals my breath
I panic
Afraid of what is happening
But still in love
Still amazed

Playful and wanting more
Till the day there is nothing
But cold days and empty trees
Wondering why can't
It last one more day
How is it that the season is over?
You are my autumn
The season I love

I am me

I remember
Even if you don't
I can breathe even through your smoke
I smile
Whether you try to wipe it off my face
I see
There is light in the dark
I dream
When all is lost

My arms will never be held
You can't hold me down
My spirit has wings
They lift me off the ground
You can't burn my feet
When I walk through the ring of fire you lit
Trying to keep me from choosing my own path
I walk on water
When you try to drown me in the ocean

I am me
That's who I choose to be
Thank you
For making it easy
By you blocking me
You should have known

I take the path with the most stones
The one that seems unclear
The one that needs gear, boots and a strong will
You pretty much pushed me over that hill

Some day you will forgive me
I'll be there for that hug
That knowing smile
That heart that never forgets

When others cover their tracks
Wipe away their foot prints
I leave mine for everyone to see

You can disagree with me
Yell till your blue in your face
Try to make me look at my mistakes

I know where I have been
How I have gotten there
Whom I have loved
And hurt along the way

I don't hide my wrongs
Pretend I'm something I'm not
I don't ask for more then I have
I'm ok with whatever I got
I dream of having more
But don't regret not getting there

Things change
Plans become new
There may be what if's
But never
I should have

I am who I have become
For your help
I thank thee

Your love I hold dear
With all love stored away
Never forgetting where I have been
Whom I have loved
Why
I am me

My Mentor

Out of the dark shadows you pulled me
Looking at me like no one ever has
Breaking down walls that took years to build
Cutting away all the evil
Hugging me and daring anyone to mess with me
Your energy circling me
Safe behind the sign you hung around me

You gave me strength to look people in the eyes
again
Not to fear what I read in their faces
People wondered what was happening
Where were my insecurities

The sadness fading
Confidence building within
Losing people out of misunderstanding
Not knowing what I was doing
Trying hard to heal

My head spinning and tears rolling
Wanting a dark corner to hide in
Harder then I thought
Liking the shadows better
Wishing I never met you
Losing all connections
Not knowing what world I belonged in
Trying to build up walls again
Breaking into pieces
With no one to pick them up

I just want to be happy
You gave it to me
Then took it away
Not understanding anything anymore
I can't turn
I won't look back
I can't block people out

I just need what I'm looking for
Maybe what I searched for
Was never what I seek
The answers are in my own mind
Thank you

Reflection

Closing my eyes
Taking a deep breath
Signing with great impact
I try to clear my mind
To focus

Am I where I should be?
Standing here
Waiting for life to hit me

What I believe
And what you see
 Are different to me

I can hear
The voice inside me
Telling me
I am
Where I should be

Hello to me!

Bye

I knew you would point out my faults
Someday you would break my heart
I can't help but know
That
Some things will go wrong

You didn't care about me
As much as you said
An act
A game to you
Waiting for something better

Feeling used
How could I be such a fool?
Maybe one day you will regret it

Be sorry
You didn't want me
I could have been happy with you

You have made your choice
Now I have made mine
Bye

Poison to my soul

Close to tears
Almost done
I want to drink to feel numb
I hate you
And love you more
Your poison to my soul
You make me sick and weak
I feel like I need a bed
I have gone crazy
Will you be happy now?
Knowing you have ruined me?
Don't you get it?
I love you more!
You never loved me best!
If you had
I wouldn't be here
Feeling sad
What makes you always right?
Why am I wrong?
I'm the one who kept you strong!
Are you happy now?
You have made me cry!
Your poison to my soul

I'm sorry

I'm sorry
Sorry for being mean
Having walls
Blocking you out
Needing you to tell me you love me
50 times a day
But still not believing you
Sorry for my doubts
The pedestal you think
I put myself on
Sorry for believing everything
People say about me
Sorry you opened up and closed again
And I did the same
Sorry for telling you I hate you
Not saying I love you enough
Sorry for my emptiness
My sorrow
I'm sorry for everything I have ever said
Sorry for looking for something better
I'm sorry for the times
I didn't think we would make it
I'm sorry you think and thought
I didn't care
Sorry for having too many opinions
My lack of love
Sorry for making you think
I was using you
I'm sorry I don't keep friends
I'm just so sorry
I'm sorry I make you sad
Sorry for picking you up
And then knocking you down

Sorry I miss my home
And don't want to move away
Sorry I broke your heart
I'm sorry we fight
I'm sorry I care what our family's think
Sorry I can't love myself
That I behave badly
I'm Sorry